FIRST-PERSON STORIES OF THE VIETNAM WAR

BY NICOLE HORNING

ROSEN PUBLISHING PRIMARY SOURCE LIBRARY

ROSEN PUBLISHING

Published in 2027 by The Rosen Publishing Group, Inc.
2544 Clinton Street, Buffalo, NY 14224

Designer: Deanna Lepovich
Editor: Nicole Horning

Cataloging-in-Publication Data

Names: Horning, Nicole.
Title: First-person stories of the Vietnam War / Nicole Horning.
Description: Buffalo, NY : Rosen Publishing, 2027. | Series: The Rosen Publishing primary source library | Includes glossary and index.
Identifiers: ISBN 9781725342927 (pbk.) | ISBN 9781725342934 (library bound) | ISBN 9781725342941 (ebook)
Subjects: LCSH: Vietnam War, 1961-1975--Juvenile literature. | Vietnam War, 1961-1975--United States--Juvenile literature.
Classification: LCC DS557.7 H67 2027 | DDC 959.7043--dc23

Manufactured in the United States of America

CPSIA Compliance Information: Batch #CSRYA27. For further information, contact Rosen Publishing at 1-800-237-9932.

CONTENTS

FOREWORD

History is so much more than just a boring collection of names and dates. It is a collection of stories—sometimes tragic stories, sometimes heroic stories, sometimes romantic stories, sometimes scary stories. And they're all stories of real people who lived real lives.

Those stories can get lost in the shuffle of memorizing battles, studying maps, and listing important court cases or rulers. That's why primary sources are so valuable. They remind us that historical events happened to and because of real people. Reading diaries, looking at photographs, and seeing newspaper articles are just some ways to make history feel personal through primary sources.

Another way is through watching or listening to interviews with people who lived through major historical events. That's what you're invited to do in this book—and all the books that are part of *The Rosen Publishing Primary Source Library*. Each chapter includes quotes from an interview with a real person who experienced a major historical event in a deeply personal way. You can also scan the QR code included at the beginning of each chapter to watch a video interview with the person featured in that chapter.

Created in partnership with Generations Broadcasting, *The Rosen Publishing Primary Source Library* was created to remind readers that there is power in sharing our stories. First-person stories make history come alive. And when history comes alive, we're better able to learn from it—and avoid the mistakes of the past.

The events you're living through today will be part of the next generation's history lessons. As you read and watch the stories collected here, think about what you want your story to be.

Note: More interviews about the topics featured in this series, as well as many other historical events, can be accessed via a subscription to Rosen Publishing's GBC Stories Database: rosendigital.com/GBCStories/.

HOW TO WATCH THE INTERVIEWS FEATURED IN THIS BOOK

- Use your phone's camera, and hold it over the QR code.
- Click the link that appears.
- Watch the video that pops up. If you would like to read a transcript of the interview while you watch, you can click on that option next to the video screen.

INTRODUCTION

The Vietnam War was one of the longest and most divided wars in American history. It started as a struggle within Vietnam, but quickly grew into a larger conflict that divided the United States.

The war began in about 1954, after the French were defeated at Dien Bien Phu. This divided the country into communist North Vietnam, led by Ho Chi Minh, and U.S.-backed South Vietnam, led by Ngo Dinh Diem. However, while this was the official start of the Vietnam War, conflict in the area actually went back several decades. The French loss at Dien Bien Phu ended nearly a century of French rule in Indochina (an area consisting of Vietnam, Laos, and Cambodia).

After this defeat, world leaders met to decide what would happen next. Many people in Vietnam wanted to self-rule, but the Cold War (a geopolitical rivalry between the United States and Soviet Union, beginning in about 1947 and ending in 1991) shaped this struggle. The United States and Soviet Union were both competing for influence, and U.S. leaders believed in the "domino theory": if one country fell to communism, nearby countries may quickly follow.

In the years that followed, fighting increased between North and South Vietnam. Communist fighters, known as the Viet Cong, tried to overthrow the government in South Vietnam. The United States initially sent military advisors to help train South Vietnamese troops. However, after U.S. ships were attacked in the Gulf of Tonkin in 1964, President Lyndon B. Johnson was given permission to expand military action and hundreds of thousands of soldiers were sent into Vietnam.

The war was fought in difficult conditions such as dense jungles and unfamiliar terrain. Additionally, guerrilla warfare made it hard for American troops to identify the enemy. Footage of combat was shown on TVs in America, and protests broke out across the country. Many people believed the war wasn't necessary or winnable.

After several years of fighting and growing opposition against the war in America, U.S. forces began to withdraw in the early 1970s. In 1975, North Vietnamese troops captured Saigon, which officially

A map of Vietnam and its neighbors, Laos and Cambodia, is shown here.

ended the war and united Vietnam under communist control. But the effects of the war didn't end there. More than 58,000 American service members died, with nearly 18,000 of those being draftees who didn't choose to join the military. Many military members returned home with physical and emotional wounds that would never really go away. The war's impact on veterans, families, and U.S. foreign policy lasted for decades, remaining one of the most debated periods in history.

CHAPTER ONE

THE WAR BEGINS: SOLDIER DRAFTING AND TRAINING

When the United States increased its involvement in the Vietnam War, it needed hundreds of thousands of soldiers to fight overseas. Some men volunteered, but many others were required to serve through the draft. In an interview with a Vietnam War veteran, the veteran discussed being drafted into the military and the difficult training process he had to go through.

BEING DRAFTED

The Selective Service System, or the draft, was started in 1948 and required men between the ages of 18 and 26 to register for 21 months of active military duty. At first, the draft was considered a "peacetime" draft, which meant the nation wasn't officially at war and was using the draft to maintain military readiness. In his interview, the Vietnam veteran described being drafted:

> *I didn't join [the military]. I married September the 17th, 1960. I was drafted December the 24th, 1960, just a few months later. I'm saying they won't take me. We had to go to Dallas for physicals. I said, they won't take me. I said, I'm married and they want the big boys, you know? [My wife] cried and cried.*

Scan this QR code to watch a Vietnam veteran discuss being drafted into the military and what training was like.

As the United States joined the war in Vietnam, protests spread across the nation, with veterans from other wars joining them.

> **FAST FACT**
>
> ABOUT 25%, OR 2.2 MILLION, OF THOSE WHO SERVED IN VIETNAM WERE DRAFTED BETWEEN 1964 AND 1973.

Thousands of men were called into service, even if they had just started new jobs, gotten married, or started families. Families were given little time to prepare while facing the fear of separation and uncertainty of war. While some men volunteered for the military out of a sense of patriotism or duty, others felt **anxious** about being sent to fight in a conflict far from home.

VIETNAM-ERA SOLDIER TRAINING

Vietnam-era training was tough, to prepare soldiers for what they had to do and encounter if sent to Vietnam. As soon as soldiers arrived at training, they were given a military haircut, and their possessions were taken away and replaced with military-issue items. In his interview, a Vietnam veteran discussed how difficult training was:

> *I remember getting on that bus and driving to Dallas and taking that physical. There's a town called Killeen outside of Waco*

While there were a lot of protests during the Vietnam War, many of them remained peaceful, with signs demanding peace instead of war.

FAST FACT

THE AVERAGE AGE OF MEN WHO WERE DRAFTED DROPPED FROM 23 YEARS OF AGE EARLY IN THE WAR TO 20 YEARS OF AGE BY 1966.

where Fort Hood is in, not too far from there. And I got off that night at 10:30, hadn't eaten all day, got off the bus, and a little old sergeant stood on both of my feet, cussed me up from one side and down and said, you are mine. Well, I was his for eight weeks, and that killed me. We were in such good shape by the end of eight weeks ...We could jog 8 miles [12.9 km] out and 8 miles back with 80-pound [36.3 kg] packs and rifle and steel helmet on our heads. They were gearing up for Vietnam, so that's why they were making all the training tough.

[The reality] began to sink in when they'd wake you up at three o'clock in the morning and run you out there and you had to do all your ***calisthenics****. And then if you couldn't chin up fifteen times, you didn't eat. When you did make it into the mess hall, the tables [had] four men sit at each table and a sergeant would go in between 'em with a stick and bang on that table and say, "eat and get out," bang, "eat and get out."*

Military training got soldiers used to carrying a lot of items on them as they hiked through tall grasses and rice paddies like the soldiers shown here.

The first eight weeks of training focused on basic combat training (also known as boot camp) while the next nine weeks was advanced individual training. Training included hand-to-hand combat, using different types of rifles, simulated combat conditions, endurance exercises, and more. There was also specialized combat for different army divisions and roles. For example, the U.S. Navy received firefighting training, and pilots received flight training. The Vietnam War had a larger need for helicopters than previous wars the United States had been in because they were used as transportation for troops, supplies, and weapons, as air ambulances, and as attack weapons. Because of this, there was a large need for pilots.

GULF OF TONKIN INCIDENT

For the first 10 years of the Vietnam War, the United States had advisors in Vietnam but didn't escalate to full combat operations. That changed with the Gulf of Tonkin incident in August 1964. From August 2 to 4, North Vietnamese torpedo boats made two attacks on U.S. ships *Maddox* and *Turner Joy*. These attacks led to the Gulf of Tonkin Resolution, in which President Lyndon B. Johnson used

DRAFT DODGING

The draft was one of the most controversial parts of the Vietnam War. Many men and families felt anxious, angry, and confused about being forced to enlist in the military. Many people said it placed an unfair burden on young men, while others believed it was necessary to supply soldiers. These feelings were even more painful for families who didn't agree with the war or American involvement in it. As a result of these feelings, draft resistance and draft dodging hit an all-time high during the Vietnam War.

About 170,000 men classified themselves as **Conscientious** Objectors (COs), which allowed them to avoid combatant military service. At first, CO status needed a religious justification but in 1965 and 1970, the reasoning expanded to include deeply held ethical or moral beliefs against all wars. Applicants often needed extensive documentation and interviews with local draft boards to qualify.

Others simply didn't report for induction into the military when called or tried to claim that they had a disability. Some fled to Canada through a network of anti-war supporters. Starting in 1964, college students started burning their draft cards as an act of protest.

About 100,000 men fled the United States to Canada or Sweden because they had more **lenient** penalties for draft dodgers, and many who went to Canada ended up staying there. Men who were draft dodging and ended up being caught could face up to five years in prison

FAST FACT

BY MAY 1965, IT BECAME MORE COMMON FOR YOUNG MEN TO DESTROY OR BURN THEIR DRAFT CARDS, SO IN AUGUST 1965, IT BECAME A FEDERAL OFFENSE TO KNOWINGLY DESTROY A DRAFT CARD.

these attacks to send many more troops into Vietnam as well as justify sustained bombing in North Vietnam.

On August 2, the *Maddox* was approached by three North Vietnamese torpedo boats. The U.S. ship fired three warning shots, and the torpedo boats continued, but the *Maddox* called in air support. This made the United States believe that North Vietnam was targeting a mission to gather information, so the *Turner Joy* was then sent in to reinforce

One group of desert-

One common form of protest during the Vietnam War was to burn draft cards. As this protest became more common, it also became a federal offense to do so.

and heavy fines. However, convictions were rare and in 1977, President Jimmy Carter pardoned most Vietnam War draft evaders. This pardon did not include deserters who left the military after joining, however.

One group of deserters known as the Intrepid Four didn't return to their ship after a daylong shore leave. They destroyed their identification and military uniforms and connected with a Japanese peace group, who would go on to help nearly 20 other American deserters.

the *Maddox*. On August 4, both ships reported being tracked from multiple unidentified vessels and began to fire at these vessels. However, information later came out that there actually wasn't an attack on August 4.

In response to the attack, Congress passed the Gulf of Tonkin Resolution, stating that the president was allowed to take all necessary measures to **repel** armed attacks against American forces and prevent further

President Lyndon B. Johnson, shown here, issued the Gulf of Tonkin Resolution to increase U.S. forces in Vietnam.

problems. Because the war intensified in 1965, many more troops were needed, so the military had to rely on the draft to fill ranks.

WATCHING DRAFT NUMBERS ON TV

As the need for more troops increased, many more men needed to be drafted. In response to this, the draft changed in a dramatic way in 1969. For the first time, the government held a televised draft lottery to decide who would be called to serve. In December of 1969, birth dates were drawn at random on live television. Each date was assigned a number between 1 and 366. Men whose birthdays matched the lower numbers were more likely to be drafted, while those with higher numbers were less likely to be called.

Families across the country anxiously watched their TVs to find out which dates were chosen first. The lottery was designed to make the draft seem fairer, but **discrimination** still existed in the system. Throughout the war, Black men were drafted at higher rates than white men in the early years, and men from low-income families were more likely to be sent into combat roles. College students, who were often from wealthier families, could receive deferments that postponed their service, while working-class men without access to higher education had fewer

The draft started being televised in 1969. This photo shows the first capsule number being drawn.

As the war continued and more young men were drafted, families became increasingly worried about the Vietnam War and wanted it to end.

options. As a result, many people said that the burden of war didn't fall equally on all Americans.

HOW YOU SEE HISTORY

1. Do you think the draft was fair? Why or why not?
2. Some groups of people were drafted at higher rates than others. How might this have increased anger and protests during the war?
3. How did the draft affect soldiers as well as their families at home?

CHAPTER TWO

THE REALITY OF WAR

The moment soldiers stepped off a plane into Vietnam, they were hit with intense heat, thick humidity, and even enemy fire. Even with the intense training they had done before entering Vietnam, the landscape was unlike anything they had trained for, consisting of dense jungles, flooded rice paddies, and enemies sometimes dressed as civilians. At the same time, Americans at home watched the war on their TVs, worried about their loved ones fighting the war or worrying about them being drafted. In an interview with Harold Culver, a Vietnam veteran, he described what it was like to land in Vietnam and immediately be a part of the combat.

WHAT IT WAS LIKE FOR SOLDIERS LANDING IN VIETNAM

Vietnam was shocking for many soldiers who were arriving there. Not only were many young men drafted into the war instead of volunteering, but they were also landing in an area with overwhelming heat (sometimes 100 degrees Fahrenheit (27 degrees Celsius)) and 100 percent humidity, which made it feel even hotter. In addition to this, there was the constant smell of rotting vegetation and jet fuel as well as chaotic combat.

Scan this QR code to watch Harold Culver discuss what it was like to land in Vietnam and experience fighting.

Vietnam was covered with thick jungles, which made it difficult to fight because the area was unknown and it was easy for enemy forces to hide.

For many soldiers landing in Vietnam, the experience was terrifying, especially if landing in a combat zone. Soldiers would have to jump from a hovering helicopter right into dense, wet, and tall foliage while under fire. Soldiers often felt **vulnerable** right away in Vietnam because they were in an unfamiliar area with thick jungles, watery rice paddies, and hostile residents. This meant the environment was a lot more unpredictable and chaotic than anyone had expected. Harold Culver described what it was like to land in Vietnam and immediately experience combat:

How I was introduced to Vietnam, we got off the plane, and the sergeant was standing there with a clipboard and a list of names and he was telling us to line up over here and we called roll call, see who he had who he didn't have. In the midst of him calling that roll call, we got incoming, which is the enemy shooting mortars and rockets at us. And it was hitting all over around that air base. And he told us to run and follow him and he took off running. We followed him, we ran into a bunker, and we stayed

Vietnam's climate is very hot and humid, which was overwhelming for soldiers landing in this new area. A blanket of fog is shown here over the mountains in Vietnam.

there until about 30 minutes until it was over with. And that was my introduction to Vietnam.

For many soldiers, this chaos wasn't unusual. It set the tone for what the rest of their time in the war would be like.

FAST FACT

VIETNAM IS THE MOST HEAVILY BOMBED COUNTRY IN HISTORY. THE UNITED STATES DROPPED MORE THAN 7.5 MILLION TONS OF BOMBS ON VIETNAM, LAOS, AND CAMBODIA IN LESS THAN 10 YEARS. THIS IS MORE THAN TRIPLE WHAT WAS USED IN WORLD WAR II.

The climate itself was one of the greatest challenges soldiers experienced. The intense heat drained energy quickly, and the heavy humidity made tasks exhausting. During **monsoon** season, heavy rains flooded fields and turned the ground into thick mud. Clothing and boots were almost always wet, which led to painful infections and diseases like **trench foot**. Staying dry and healthy was nearly impossible.

LIFE IN VIETNAM

The jungle terrain added even more danger for soldiers. The thick vegetation made it very difficult for soldiers to move, so it was nearly impossible to see enemies. Soldiers had to constantly watch for booby traps such as sharpened stakes and trip wires connected to explosives. Mosquitoes swarmed in the humid air

FAST FACT

HELICOPTER WARFARE, OR "AIR MOBILITY," STARTED IN 1965 AND REVOLUTIONIZED COMBAT. HELICOPTERS WERE USED FOR MEDICAL EVACUATION, COMBAT SUPPORT, AND RAPID DEPLOYMENT OF TROOPS.

Vietnam's terrain presented many challenges, including accessing supplies. Because jungle cover was so thick, it was hard for helicopters to drop off supplies, so crew had to offload supplies from the air such as in this photo.

THE VIETNAM WAR IN POPULAR CULTURE

The Vietnam War influenced popular culture in a way that previous wars hadn't. For the first time, Americans could watch the war unfold on the TV nearly every night. News programs aired footage from the battlefield, such as helicopters landing in rice paddies, soldiers carrying other wounded soldiers, and villages damaged from the fighting. Because people could see these images right in their living room, the war no longer felt far away. Because of this and the draft, the war became personal.

Music became a powerful form of expression during that time, with many songs questioning the war and government policies. Bob Dylan's song "Masters of War" expressed intense anger toward people who started wars. Creedence Clearwater Revival's song "Fortunate Son" is one of the most popular anti-Vietnam War protest songs, motivated by the unfairness of the draft. "Fortunate Son" has been featured in many movies to represent the Vietnam War era and is often featured in scenes with helicopters, such as in the movie *Forrest Gump*.

Billy Joel's song "Goodnight Saigon" focused on the soldier's experience rather than making a political statement. The lyrics spoke about brotherhood and the lack of support soldiers received when returning from Vietnam. The song followed the journey from training through fighting in Vietnam and then returning home. Joel wrote the song after talking with veterans who felt that their experiences weren't recognized or understood.

Other songs associated with the Vietnam War, protests, and soldier experience include "War" by Edwin Starr, "Paint It, Black" by the Rolling Stones, "All Along the Watchtower" by Jimi Hendrix, "We Gotta Get Out of This Place" by The Animals, and "For What It's Worth" by Buffalo Springfield. These songs and many others were frequently played on military radio, becoming a type of soundtrack for the war. To this day, these songs are still associated with the Vietnam War and are featured in movies with scenes of the Vietnam War.

In 2007 the movie *Across the Universe* was released with a soundtrack of Beatles' covers. The movie used these songs to highlight how unstable society was during the Vietnam War era and showed soldiers being drafted as well as volunteering to join, soldier injuries, anti-Vietnam War protests, funerals for soldiers, and the lasting impacts of the war on veterans.

Bases consisted of several barracks. A living area for soldiers is shown here.

and leeches would cling to skin during marches through swamps and rice paddies.

Beyond the physical challenges soldiers faced, many of them also experienced culture shock. The language, food, and customs were unfamiliar. Some civilians were friendly, but others supported the North Vietnamese forces. This made it difficult to tell who was a civilian or an enemy fighter, making soldiers feel uneasy even when not in direct combat.

FAST FACT

"DUSTOFF" MEDICS CARED FOR PATIENTS DURING THE FLIGHT AND KEPT THEM ALIVE UNTIL THEY ARRIVED AT A HOSPITAL AND SURGICAL UNIT FOR CARE. MEDICS AND DUSTOFF TEAMS TRANSPORTED MORE THAN 900,000 WOUNDED SOLDIERS TO HOSPITALS, OFTEN WITHIN 15 MINUTES.

One of the combat tactics used in Vietnam was trench warfare, in which soldiers would dig trenches to protect themselves from artillery and machine-gun fire.

Life in Vietnam also depended on if a soldier was stationed at a base camp or in the field. At base camps, soldiers had tents or barracks, regular meals, and rest between missions. However, attacks could happen without warning even at a base camp. Other soldiers spent days or weeks in the field, carrying heavy packs, sleeping on the ground, and staying constantly alert, never knowing when fighting may start.

HOW YOU SEE HISTORY

1. How did the environment in Vietnam (such as monsoons, jungles, and humidity) impact how soldiers experienced the war?
2. How would constant vigilance and an inability to clearly identify who the enemy was affect a soldier's emotions and ability to make decisions?
3. Why did guerrilla warfare make it difficult for soldiers to feel safe, even when they weren't in active combat?

CHAPTER THREE

THE WAR ESCALATES

By 1968, the Vietnam War reached a turning point with major surprise attacks, supply routes, and chemical warfare. New technology changed how the war was fought, while at home the war created divisions, and the number of protests escalated. An interview with veteran David Maxfield discusses new technology used during the Vietnam War and why it was so dangerous.

THE TET OFFENSIVE

In the early hours of January 1968, 85,000 North Vietnamese troops attacked five major cities, several towns and villages, and many military installations in South Vietnam at the same time. North Vietnamese and the Viet Cong had approximately 60,000 **casualties** while the Americans and South Vietnamese had more than 12,000 casualties, including 2,600 fatalities. Although the attack was a crushing defeat for the North, it reduced American support for the Vietnam War even more.

The Tet Offensive showed that the North Vietnamese were still able to organize large and powerful attacks. In the United States, images on TV showed combat inside of cities and at the U.S. Embassy in Saigon. These images contradicted earlier statements

Scan this QR code to watch David Maxfield talk about fighting tactics during the war and an injury he almost received.

An infantry unit is shown here moving through the jungle in Vietnam.

FAST FACT

THE VIETNAM WAR WAS A "TELEVISION WAR" BECAUSE IT WAS THE FIRST HEAVILY TELEVISED WAR. THIS MADE IT SIGNIFICANTLY IMPACT PUBLIC OPINION ON THE WAR AND ALSO INCREASED OPPOSITION TO THE WAR AS IT DRAGGED ON.

that victory was near, which made Americans start to doubt official reports. As a result, public support declined sharply and political leaders faced increasing pressure to change course and leave Vietnam.

TECHNOLOGY IN THE WAR

The Vietnam War was the most technologically advanced war up to that time. New chemical weapons, powerful aircraft, and **modern** equipment were all used to gain an advantage, but it didn't always guarantee success. David Maxfield, a Vietnam War veteran, described his role in communications:

Our role was to support the various artillery batteries out in the field, and they would drop you off in the evening. Typically, it would be me and an officer, they would drop us off. We'd walk up on top of a hill [and] the next day we would observe a valley to see if there's any enemy movement. That night we would walk to another hill, observe for a day, and then do that. Typically you're out three nights. They had an extraction point for you where they were gonna pick you up that last day, and then if there was anything going on in between there, you could call for

Marines move into a village after several days of heavy fighting with North Vietnam forces.

an extraction immediately. In the Tet of 68, the Viet Cong were **decimated** *in the south, but the North Vietnamese army took on a much larger role, and they had what they called directional antennas. So if you're on a radio talking, if you talk too long, they could take these antennas and* **triangulate** *you, get a decent idea of where you were.*

Communication technology was critical in Vietnam. Radios allowed soldiers to call for support, airstrikes, or medical evacuation, and helicopters could extract troops quickly. However, the North Vietnamese army and Viet Cong adapted. They used antennas to locate radio signals, allowing them to find the U.S. and South Vietnamese troops if radios were used too long.

Beginning in 1965, the United States started relying heavily on helicopters. Helicopters transported troops into remote areas, delivered supplies, and evacuated the wounded, while fighter jets dropped bombs on areas where the enemy was and supply routes.

A river boat is shown here spraying napalm, which is a highly flammable substance.

Napalm, a sticky and flammable substance, was used to destroy the jungle and enemy areas. When napalm ignited, it burned at very high temperatures and couldn't be easily put out.

Another chemical used was Agent Orange, which was sprayed from aircraft to remove dense jungle cover. The military believed that removing trees would reveal enemy supply routes and reduce ambushes. However, Agent Orange was made up of toxic chemicals that later caused major health problems such as cancer, and many American veterans developed illnesses related to exposure to Agent Orange.

FAST FACT

THE UNITED STATES USED ABOUT 20 MILLION GALLONS (76 MILLION LITERS) OF AGENT ORANGE TO DESTROY FOREST AND FARMLAND IN VIETNAM.

U.S. Army members are shown here spraying Agent Orange, which is a very toxic substance that caused health problems years later.

PROTESTS DURING THE VIETNAM WAR

The Vietnam War is the most **sustained** protest movement in history, involving campus protests, draft **resistance**, and marches. Many people, especially college students, questioned why the United States was involved in the Vietnam War. Some believed the government wasn't being fully honest while others opposed the draft because they believed that it was unfairly requiring young men to serve, especially during a **volatile** and long-running war.

College students organized marches and rallies, carrying signs, singing songs, and demanding an end to the war. While many protests were peaceful, sometimes they escalated, such as at Kent State University in Ohio.

During a 1970 protest at the university, 28 National Guard troops fired approximately 67 rounds within 13 seconds into a crowd of more than 300 students. The guards ended up killing four and wounding

Students are shown running away from tear gas that National Guard members were using during the Kent State protests.

nine, with one suffering from permanent **paralysis**. Photographs of the event quickly spread, shocking the nation and showing how divided the country had become because of the war. The shootings led to outrage and even more protests and walk-outs at many high schools, colleges, and universities.

Civil rights leaders like Martin Luther King Jr. also spoke out against the Vietnam War, calling it an unjust war that drained resources from anti-poverty programs and harmed **marginalized** communities.

The protests showed how divided the war was between younger and older generations. Older generations were more likely to support the war or trust government leadership while younger generations were against the war.

National Guard members killed four students and injured nine at the Kent State protests. A student is shown here yelling for help during the protest.

Napalm bombs are shown here exploding south of Saigon in Vietnam.

GUERRILLA WARFARE

Much of the fighting in Vietnam was guerrilla warfare, which involved surprise attacks, small groups of fighters, and knowledge of local terrain instead of large, traditional battlefields. Additionally, the Viet Cong and North Vietnamese often relied on hit-and-run tactics, attacking quickly, often at night, and then fleeing into the jungle before American troops could respond.

Booby traps were one of the most feared weapons used in guerrilla warfare. Tripwires could trigger grenades, and hidden pits lined with sharpened stakes were placed along jungle paths. Even everyday objects could be rigged with explosives. These traps injured thousands of soldiers and created constant anxiety.

Another challenge was the use of tunnel systems such as the Cu Chi Tunnel system north of Ho Chi Minh City. The Viet Cong used

An entryway of the Cu Chi Tunnel system is shown here.

this 155-mile (250 km) to house troops, supply routes, and hospitals. This tunnel system was an essential part of the Viet Cong's surprise attacks against American forces. North Vietnam also relied on a complex supply network called the Ho Chi Minh Trail, which was 12,000 miles (19,312 km) long. This was made up of paths, roads, and waterways through neighboring Laos and Cambodia. The pathway avoided the heavily defended border, allowing it to bypass U.S. blockades so that trucks, bicycles, and porters could carry weapons and supplies south.

The United States bombed sections of this trail repeatedly, but it was difficult to stop because the network constantly moved and was repaired by 300,000 full-time workers. If one route was destroyed, another was built. This allowed North Vietnamese forces to continue fighting, even after heavy losses.

One of the most frustrating parts of guerrilla warfare was the inability to identify the enemy. Viet Cong fighters didn't always wear uniforms, so they might appear as farmers or villagers. This led to confusion and mistrust among American troops because they didn't know which civilians they could truly trust and when, where, or if an attack may happen. Soldiers described living in **perpetual**

A section of the narrow Cu Chi Tunnels is shown here.

> **FAST FACT**
>
> THE VIETNAM WAR CAUSED MORE THAN 3 MILLION DEATHS, INCLUDING MORE THAN 58,000 U.S. MILITARY MEMBERS.

vigilance. They would constantly scan their surroundings and listen for unusual sounds. This awareness took a severe toll on soldiers' emotions. However, this **stress** wasn't limited to combat roles. Nurses and medical staff also experienced extreme

Medics and helicopters were essential for saving many lives during combat. A medic is shown here waiting for a medevac for a wounded soldier.

trauma from treating thousands of soldiers with severe burns, gunshot wounds, and other life-threatening injuries every day. Helicopters regularly transported wounded soldiers away from the battlefield, sometimes faster than medical teams could keep up.

HOW YOU SEE HISTORY

1. Why is the Tet Offensive considered a turning point in the Vietnam War?
2. Why do you think younger and older generations disagreed about the Vietnam War?
3. How did communication technology protect as well as endanger soldiers in the Vietnam War?

CHAPTER FOUR

THE HUMAN COST

Vietnam was a confusing landscape, but the way combat was fought made it even more confusing. Days could be tense but quiet while nights brought rocket fire and surprise attacks. Holidays that were meant to be peaceful were actually filled with attacks. As a result of this, the Vietnam War took a large toll on mental and emotional health, leading to significant stress and making soldiers feel constantly alert. In an interview with a Vietnam War veteran, the veteran described how confusing the war was from the moment he landed.

FIGHTING AFTER DARK

Vietnam was a confusing, unknown territory, and this started right when soldiers landed. In an interview, a Vietnam veteran described what it was like landing in the area and his immediate confusion:

We landed in Vietnam and it's comical now, but it wasn't then. We're all in our flak jackets and helmets and packs and making a landing, which is what we're accustomed to or trained to do. We go rolling into Cam Ranh Bay, and there are Navy guys on the ships looking at us and

Scan this QR code to watch a Vietnam veteran talk about landing in Vietnam and being part of a battle.

Vietnam was a confusing, unknown territory filled with dense jungle cover that troops had to walk through.

laughing, and we were wondering, "Is this the war?" And what we didn't realize is that nothing really happened until after dark.

And then after dark is when we found out there were rockets and both going and incoming taking place.

During the day, bases would often be calm. But at night, everything changed, which made the soldiers feel **disoriented**. At night, the North Vietnamese army and Viet Cong would launch rockets and surprise attacks relying on intense firepower and **stealth**. The attacks were designed for maximum impact and psychological distress, keeping South Vietnamese and U.S. forces on edge. The North Vietnamese and Viet Cong had an advantage in the darkness. It was harder to see movement, more difficult to aim accurately, and hard to

FAST FACT

CAM RANH BAY WAS A MAJOR U.S. MILITARY BASE IN SOUTH VIETNAM. IT SERVED AS AN IMPORTANT PORT AND SUPPLY CENTER THROUGHOUT THE WAR.

The United States dropped millions of tons of bombs on Vietnam, Laos, and Cambodia during the war.

A combat team is shown here in Vietnam.

know where the danger was coming from. Because of this, sleep was often interrupted and soldiers became exhausted.

THE CHRISTMAS TRUCE

During the Vietnam War, Christmas truces were called. During these truces, for 24 to 48 hours, there wouldn't be any airstrikes

Helicopters such as the one shown here were critical to fighting the Vietnam War due to the difficult terrain.

Soldiers are shown here leaving a helicopter for a combat mission.

FAST FACT

MEDEVAC HELICOPTERS TRANSPORTED WOUNDED SOLDIERS FROM THE BATTLEFIELD TO MEDICAL FACILITIES. FAST EVACUATION INCREASED SURVIVAL RATES FOR INJURED SOLDIERS.

or ground attacks. However, the peace these truces were supposed to bring about was uneasy because soldiers constantly felt alert, and there were still some attacks from both sides. In his interview, the Vietnam veteran described the Christmas truce while he was there and how it wasn't very peaceful:

> *We had convoy from Dong Ha to a place called Cam Lo and we were up there to support an infantry...and two days before Christmas, the so-called Christmas Truce, is when we got hit pretty hard. And we lost a few of our guys. And quite a few injured. And they had to be medevac.*

Even during a holiday that should have been a break from the fighting, there was still danger, and this showed how unpredictable the war was. For U.S. troops who were far from home, holidays were

U.S. Special Forces teams are shown here on a combat patrol mission in Vietnam.

made even more difficult because they were reminded of family celebrations that they were missing. When attacks happened during these times, it made the holidays even harder.

VIETNAMESE CIVILIANS

The war had a significant impact on soldiers, but Vietnamese civilians were also caught in the middle of fighting. Many villages were located in areas where both sides were. Civilians often faced pressure to provide food, shelter, or information.

Some people fled their homes to escape violence and became refugees. They moved to larger cities or temporary camps, often leaving behind belongings, farms, and animals. These refugee camps were often overcrowded and had poor sanitation. Many people spent months or years in camps with these conditions.

One of the most tragic events involving civilians was the My Lai Massacre in March 1968. During a search-and-destroy mission, U.S. troops entered the village of My Lai. However, many of the people

WHAT FAMILIES KNEW OF VIETNAM

The war was a constant source of worry for families. Communication wasn't instant like it is today, so soldiers and their families had to rely on letters. Soldiers would write letters when they could, but slow delivery times meant that it could be weeks before families received a letter. However, the information that soldiers could share was very limited, and letters were often censored to avoid sharing sensitive information, or intercepted so that families didn't receive a letter at all. This left families with gaps in information about the true danger their loved one was facing.

Television was a main source of information because news programs showed footage such as combat scenes and reports of casualties. This meant that families would watch these reports without knowing if their loved one was nearby. When reporters announced the names of areas under attack, fear spread quickly.

Families found out their loved one had died through an informal, cold letter. The letter would be delivered unexpectedly by a local taxi driver. This policy changed between 1966 and 1967 because Julie Moore, wife of Lieutenant General Hal Moore, advocated for this impersonal policy to be changed to a more personal notification from military officers. After seeing many families receive notices through an impersonal letter and taxi driver, she wanted to make sure families had a support system and weren't alone when they found out the news.

However, even when soldiers survived, families still worried about injuries and how the war would impact their loved one emotionally and mentally. Some parents felt helpless because they couldn't protect their child from danger thousands of miles away.

in My Lai were unarmed civilians, including women, children, and the elderly. U.S. troops were ordered to enter the village firing their guns, but there weren't any reports of opposing fire. More than 300 unarmed civilians were killed in the massacre.

News of the massacre didn't reach the public until more than a year later in November 1969. As details reached the public, questions about U.S. soldiers' conduct in Vietnam were raised. An investigation found there were failures in leadership, discipline, and morale in the fighting units.

More than 300 Vietnamese civilians were killed during the My Lai Massacre.

U.S. soldiers are shown here searching through belongings after the My Lai Massacre for evidence of the Viet Cong.

FAST FACT

IT'S ESTIMATED THAT ABOUT 4 MILLION PEOPLE WERE EXPOSED TO AGENT ORANGE AND UP TO 2 MILLION OF THEM HAVE ILLNESSES RELATED TO EXPOSURE. MORE THAN 300,000 U.S. VETERANS AND 400,000 VIETNAMESE PEOPLE HAVE DIED FROM ILLNESSES RELATED TO AGENT ORANGE.

THE EMOTIONAL TOLL

Combat in Vietnam placed intense mental and physical strain on soldiers. Night attacks, unclear enemy positions, and the constant threat of ambush meant that troops often remained in a heightened state of alert. Sleep was limited and frequently interrupted. Many soldiers carried weapons even while resting because attacks could happen at any time. In his interview, the Vietnam veteran said:

I will have to say the most impressive part of that whole operation was a Navy corpsman. We had one corpsman that got hit and his hand was bleeding and he just ignored that to take care

Four of the soldiers responsible for the My Lai Massacre are shown here.

of some of the wounded. It was amazing. And it was a little bit frightening because one of the guys that was in our tent had been in the Korean War, and he used to sleep with two grenades in his hands at night...But after we got hit, I really don't know what happened to him. I don't recall seeing him again.

Bases of the huts in My Lai, such as those shown here, have been preserved as they were found after the massacre.

Medics and corpsmen often treated the wounded while still under fire themselves. Their actions helped save thousands of lives. However, beyond physical injuries, the war took a mental and emotional toll on soldiers. At the time, PTSD wasn't fully understood. Symptoms like nightmares, anxiety, and trouble adjusting to civilian life after the war was often described as just "combat fatigue" or "shell shock." Strong bonds formed between soldiers who fought together. Units depended on trust and teamwork for survival, and these relationships were essential for coping with the stress of combat. However, when fellow soldiers died, the loss could have a lasting impact.

HOW YOU SEE HISTORY

1. How might nighttime attacks and interrupted sleep have affected soldiers' decision making and morale?
2. How can high stress, exhaustion, and fear affect a person's behavior in combat situations?
3. What long-term effects might soldiers experience even after returning home?

CHAPTER FIVE

THE END OF THE VIETNAM WAR AND ITS LASTING IMPACT

As the Vietnam War continued into the late 1960s, its effects were felt far beyond the battlefield. Soldiers experienced severe physical and emotional challenges that would continue long after the war was over, and the American public was even further losing its trust in the government. During his interview, veteran Harold Culver described surprise attacks from the Viet Cong and the injuries he continues to deal with today.

INJURIES AND RECOVERY

In the later years of the Vietnam War, rocket and mortar attacks on U.S. and South Vietnamese bases were common. The North Vietnamese army and Viet Cong would attack bases to **harass** troops and deny them any safety or rest, even in secured places. In his interview, Culver shared his experience with these attacks on their bases and the injuries he has from them:

> *We'd been getting incoming rounds every morning at about 9:30, 10 o'clock, and it was just routine stuff they hit, just* ***arbitrarily*** *in different places. And the enemy really didn't have foreign observers like we did. They just aimed at stuff, pulled the trigger on it, and let it go hoping*

Scan this QR code to watch Harold Culver discuss being hit by a rocket in Vietnam.

Vietnam War veterans remember and honor those who served and were lost in the war. Many surviving veterans continue to deal with the physical and emotional toll of the war.

FAST FACT

HUNDREDS OF AMERICAN SERVICE MEMBERS WERE HELD AS PRISONERS OF WAR IN NORTH VIETNAM. MANY ENDURED HARSH CONDITIONS BEFORE BEING RELEASED AFTER THE PARIS PEACE ACCORDS.

they would hit something. Well May 5, 1968, one 22-mm rocket came in and it hit the building where my communications building was, and I was sitting at the desk decoding some information. Next thing I know...I could smell rocket fuel in the explosion... and as I smelled it, I was flying through the air and I hit the wall on the other side of the roof. And that's all I remember...it killed three guys and wounded fourteen of us and ripped open the gas and diesel fuel that these generators were running on. It caught fire [and] fuel run down to the communications building and started burning it. And I've got some real bad burns on my legs.

Even 50 years later, Harold is still dealing with these injuries. Burns often needed long hospital stays, many surgeries, and a painful recovery process.

Hundreds of thousands of soldiers were injured, with injuries including burns or amputations of a limb. Other injuries caused long-term internal damage. Whether the injury was visible or not, many veterans continued to deal with the injuries decades later. Advances in medical care helped soldiers survive wounds that may have been fatal in earlier wars, but this meant long recovery periods and lifelong health challenges.

Part of the Vietnam War Memorial in Washington, DC, is a sculpture of U.S. soldiers.

POST-TRAUMATIC STRESS DISORDER AFTER THE WAR

The constant danger caused by guerrilla warfare, unseen enemies, and intense combat had long-term effects. Many veterans later struggled with post-traumatic stress disorder (PTSD), a condition that can include flashbacks, nightmares, anxiety, and sudden bursts of anger. At the time, PTSD was not well understood, and many veterans did not receive the support they needed.

PTSD can develop after someone experiences or witnesses a traumatic event. In Vietnam, soldiers faced constant danger and were always alert and on the lookout for booby traps and wondering who was an enemy. This constant need to be alert and the **prolonged tension** affected soldiers' brains and bodies.

In the 1960s and 1970s, because PTSD wasn't fully understood, soldiers with symptoms were often told to just "move on" or "forget about it." This led to feelings of isolation because doctors, family members, and friends didn't fully understand what they had experienced. Even today, about 15 percent of Vietnam veterans still have PTSD.

Since then, doctors have learned more about PTSD and its long-term effects. Support programs for veterans have expanded, with more counseling options available. Today, there are specialized therapies available for veterans with PTSD, such as **cognitive** processing therapy, and peer support groups and group therapies are also available to help veterans with PTSD. Therapies are focused on improving the quality of life for veterans instead of just managing symptoms of PTSD. Public awareness has also grown as veterans of the Vietnam War and other more recent wars have shared their stories.

Additionally, recovery didn't end when soldiers left the hospital. They had to adapt to these injuries and also go through physical therapy and even more medical procedures. Many veterans still live with pain, limited mobility, or complications related to their injuries.

THE END OF THE VIETNAM WAR

By the late 1960s, the United States was looking for a way to reduce involvement in Vietnam. The American public was exhausted from the ongoing war that was taking the lives of thousands, with little progress made in Vietnam. To remove U.S. forces without making

President Richard Nixon, shown here, introduced the Vietnamization strategy to end U.S. involvement in the war.

it look like the United States was abandoning South Vietnam to communist forces, President Richard Nixon introduced a strategy called "Vietnamization" in November 1969. The goal of this was to equip and train South Vietnamese forces and increase their combat roles while decreasing the number of U.S. troops in Vietnam.

However, at the same time that this strategy was put in place, the Nixon administration increased U.S. involvement in other areas of Southeast Asia. For example, in April 1970, Nixon secretly gave his approval for ground invasions in Cambodia as well as a bombing campaign. Cambodia was a neutral country. Nixon said

FAST FACT

THE AVERAGE AGE OF AN AMERICAN SOLDIER KILLED IN VIETNAM WAS JUST 23 YEARS OLD. MANY SERVICE MEMBERS WERE RECENT HIGH SCHOOL GRADUATES AT JUST 17 OR 18 YEARS OF AGE.

that invading Cambodia was necessary to keep pressure on the North Vietnamese forces and Viet Cong until the Vietnamization strategy gained ground and became more popular. These actions led to more massive anti-war protests in the United States.

Nixon gradually reduced the number of troops in Vietnam from about 549,000 in 1969 to 69,000 in 1972. However, ongoing attacks made Nixon doubt his Vietnamization strategy. For example, in March 1972, the Easter Offensive showed how much the South Vietnamese relied on the United States to repel attacks from the Viet Cong and North Vietnamese army.

In January 1973, the Paris Peace Accords officially ended U.S. involvement in Vietnam. It ensured the withdrawal of the rest of the U.S. troops in Vietnam within 60 days. However, the accords didn't completely end the Vietnam War. The war continued between North and South Vietnam until the fall of Saigon in 1975, when North Vietnamese forces captured the capital city. Soon after this, Vietnam was unified under communist control.

HOW VETERANS WERE TREATED AT HOME

When U.S. troops came home, reactions were mixed. Many Americans supported the troops but opposed the war. Others were angry about the war itself and directed these feelings toward returning soldiers. Unlike veterans of World War II, Vietnam veterans were not greeted with large victory parades. Because the Vietnam War was considered a failed conflict, returning soldiers weren't treated as heroes and their return was seen as a reminder of defeat. Many soldiers were openly harassed or insulted by anti-war protesters.

Because of how soldiers were treated when they came back, they often returned quietly and changed out of their military uniforms before arriving home. Because of how the war had divided the country, returning service members felt caught in the middle of political disagreements.

It wasn't until years later that soldiers were recognized for their sacrifice, the first being in 1986 with Chicago's Vietnam Veterans Parade and then in 2017 with the establishment of the National Vietnam War Veterans Day, which occurs on March 29.

VIETNAM VETERANS MEMORIAL

In 1982, the Vietnam Veterans Memorial was dedicated in Washington, DC. The memorial honors those who died or went missing in action during the war. The main feature of the memorial is a black granite wall engraved with the names of more than 58,000

The Vietnam Veterans Memorial features granite that easily shows reflections.

Americans who died in the war. Because of how the memorial was designed, visitors see their own reflection in the memorial alongside the names.

FAST FACT

THE VIETNAM WAR WAS ONE OF THE FIRST WARS WIDELY BROADCAST ON TELEVISION. GRAPHIC IMAGES OF COMBAT HEAVILY INFLUENCED PUBLIC OPINION IN THE UNITED STATES.

The names of casualties are in the order of death instead of by their military rank. This is significant because it shows that each life matters equally. The memorial also includes a Three Serviceman statue, an In Memory plaque, a flagpole that has both the U.S. and missing-in-action flags, and a

The Vietnam Women's Memorial is shown here.

Vietnam Women's Memorial. The women's memorial shows three nurses and a wounded soldier, and the names of the eight women lost in the Vietnam War are engraved in the wall. There are also eight trees in the grove near the sculpture to represent these eight women who died.

ONGOING EFFECTS OF THE VIETNAM WAR

The effects of the Vietnam War didn't end in 1975. Veterans who were exposed to Agent Orange later developed serious health problems, such as cancer. The U.S. government eventually recognized that some of the conditions veterans faced were service-related, which allowed veterans to receive benefits.

The war also impacted foreign policy with the War Powers Act of 1973. This act limits the president's ability to send U.S. forces to combat without congressional approval. This law is designed to

The Vietnam Veterans Memorial offers paper for families to trace the names of their loved ones who are honored in the memorial.

Another part of the Vietnam Veterans Memorial in Washington, DC, features a group of soldiers.

prevent long, undeclared conflicts like the Vietnam War from happening again without additional oversight.

The Vietnam War also raised important questions about government transparency. The release of the Pentagon Papers in 1971 revealed that officials didn't always share accurate information with the public about the war's progress. As a result of this, trust in the government declined for many Americans.

The Vietnam War changed the United States politically, socially, and militarily. It was one of the longest and most controversial wars in U.S. history, and it deeply divided the country. The conflict led to new laws and reshaped how the media covers war, since coverage of the Vietnam War deeply influenced public opinions. The experiences of veterans increased awareness of PTSD, leading to the expansion of support services for veterans. Today, historians continue to study the Vietnam War to understand its lessons, and its legacy remains an important part of American history.

HOW YOU SEE HISTORY

1. Why were some Vietnam veterans treated differently from veterans of earlier wars?
2. In what ways did the Vietnam War change how Americans think about military involvement overseas?
3. How can a war continue to shape a country long after the fighting ends?

TIMELINE

THE WAR BEGINS: SOLDIER DRAFTING AND TRAINING: TIMELINE OF THE VIETNAM WAR

August 1964: The Gulf of Tonkin Incident justifies the United States fully entering the Vietnam War and sending more troops.

1964: Draftees start burning their draft cards as an act of protest.

December 1969: The first televised draft lottery occurs.

THE WAR ESCALATES: TIMELINE OF THE VIETNAM WAR

1965: The United States starts relying heavily on helicopters to fight the war, transport troops, and evacuate the injured.

January 1968: During the Tet Offensive, North Vietnamese troops attack several cities, towns, villages, and military installations, leading to thousands of casualties.

1970: An anti-Vietnam War protest turns violent, with the National Guard killing four students and wounding nine.

THE HUMAN COST: TIMELINE OF THE VIETNAM WAR

1966–1967: The policy for how families are notified of deaths changes from an impersonal letter to a personal notification from military officers.

March 1968: The My Lai Massacre results in the death of more than 300 unarmed Vietnamese civilians, including women, children, and the elderly.

THE END OF THE VIETNAM WAR AND ITS LASTING IMPACT: TIMELINE OF THE VIETNAM WAR

1969: President Richard Nixon reveals the Vietnamization policy to reduce U.S. involvement in Vietnam.

April 1970: The United States starts a bombing campaign and ground invasions in Cambodia, a neutral country.

January 1973: The Paris Peace Accords officially ends U.S. involvement in the Vietnam War.

1975: North Vietnamese forces capture Saigon, ending the Vietnam War.

GLOSSARY

anxious: Strong feelings of fear or nervousness about what might happen.
arbitrarily: Something occurring randomly rather than for any reason.
calisthenics: Exercises done to build muscle and improve flexibility.
casualties: People killed or injured in a war or accident.
cognitive: Relating to knowledge and thought.
conscientious: The desire to do what is right.
decimated: To destroy or remove a large amount of something.
discrimination: Different—usually unfair—treatment based on factors such as a person's race, age, religion, or gender.
disoriented: Confused and losing a sense of direction.
harass: To bother, intimidate, or pressure someone.
lenient: To be mild and not strict or harsh.
marginalized: People or groups who are treated as unimportant and denied equal access to opportunities or resources.
modern: Relating to present times.
monsoon: A seasonal wind, especially in the Indian Ocean and southern Asia, that affects the weather.
paralysis: Unable to move.
perpetual: Something that's never ending.
prolonged: Something continuing for a long time.
repel: Force an attacker back or away.
resistance: Refusing to accept something and prevent it by action or argument.
revolutionized: To change something a lot.
stress: Strong feelings of worry.
sustained: Something that lasts a long time.
tension: A state in which people, groups, or countries disagree with and feel anger toward each other.
trauma: Something that causes extreme emotional distress.
trench foot: A serious injury to the foot caused by exposure to cold and damp conditions, resulting in numbness, blisters, swelling, and tissue damage.
triangulate: To measure and map an area by using triangles.
vigilant: To be very aware of something.
volatile: The likelihood of changing rapidly and unpredictably, often for the worse.
vulnerable: Open to being hurt or damaged.

FOR MORE INFORMATION

BOOKS

DK Eyewitness Books. *Vietnam War: Discover the People, Places, Battles, and Weapons of America's Indochina Struggle*. New York, NY: DK Publishing, 2005.

Karnow, Stanley. *Vietnam: A History*. New York, NY: Penguin Books, 1997.

Partridge, Elizabeth. *Boots on the Ground: America's War in Vietnam*. New York, NY: Viking, 2018.

Sheehan, Neil, E.W. Kenworthy, Fox Butterfield, and Hedrick Smith. *The Pentagon Papers: The Secret History of the Vietnam War*. New York, NY: Racehorse Publishing, 2017.

Wawro, Geoffrey. *The Vietnam War: A Military History*. New York, NY: Basic Books, 2024.

WEBSITES

Vietnam War

www.britannica.com/event/Vietnam-War

Learn more about the Vietnam War, causes, casualties, and more.

Vietnam War

www.history.com/topics/vietnam-war

Explore a Vietnam War timeline, photos, and more.

Vietnam War

www.archives.gov/research/vietnam-war

Learn more about the Vietnam War through extensive documents, records, photographs, and more in the National Archives.

The Vietnam War

www.bbc.co.uk/bitesize/guides/zv7bkqt/revision/1

Explore events, reasons for entering Vietnam, reasons for U.S. failure in defeating the Viet Cong, impact of the war, and more on the BBC site.

The Vietnam War: An Overview

www.vassar.edu/the-wars-for-vietnam/vietnam-war-overview

Read more about important events in the Vietnam War.

INDEX

PHOTO CREDITS

Cover Everett Collection/Shutterstock.com; p. 7 Rainer Lesniewski/ Shutterstock.com; pp. 9, 10 rmanpv35/Shutterstock.com; p. 11 My Lai war crime photograph by Ronald L. Haeberle (6)/Wikimedia Commons; p. 13 (sidebar) Draft card burning NYC 1967/Wikimedia Commons; p. 13 Lyndon B. Johnson, photo portrait, leaning on chair, color cropped/ Wikimedia Commons; pp. 14, 15, 49 courtesy of the Library of Congress; p. 17 Rick van Leeuwen/Shutterstock.com; p. 18 NickKont/Shutterstock.com; p. 19 UH-1D drops supplies to Company D, 1st Battalion, 7th Cavalry in dense jungle/Wikimedia Commons; p. 21 Living area of the 578th Maintenance Battalion at Phu Bai Combat Base/wikimedia Commons; p. 22 Duc Huy Nguyen/Shutterstock.com; p. 24 M-48 Patton tank in Vietnam 1969/Wikimedia Commons; p. 25 127-GVB-Vietnam-M-bx16-18001497/ Wikimedia Commons; p. 26 US riverboat using napalm in Vietnam/ Wikimedia Commons; p. 27 US-Army-APC-spraying-Agent-Orange-in-Vietnam/Wikimedia Commons; p. 28 Kent State shootings/Wikimedia Commons; p. 29 Mary Ann Vecchio Kent State May 4 1970 John Filo Photograph/Wikimedia Commons; pp. 30, 33 courtesy of the National Archives; p. 31 CravenA/Shutterstock.com; p. 32 Mark Green/Shutterstock.com; p. 35 1RAR patrol in War Zone D, August 1965/Wikimedia Commons; p. 36 KaikeoSaiyasane/Shutterstock.com; p. 37 (top) "FAIRFAX Operation, Gia Dinh province, an integrated US-ARVN combat team" during the Vietnam War from, "RVNAF and US Operational Cooperation and Coordination" (page 145)-(cropped)/Wikimedia Commons; p. 37 (bottom) Huy Thoai/Shutterstock.com; p. 38 6 RAR soldiers disembark from a US Army Chinook helicopter during a 1966 combat operation in South Vietnam/Wikimedia Commons; p. 39 U. S. Special Forces patrol enters Vietnamese village – Vietnam, 1964/Wikimedia Commons; pp. 41, 44 Steve Barze/Shutterstock.com; p. 42 My Lai war crime photograph by Ronald L. Haeberle (7)/Wikimedia Commons; p. 43 U.S. Army personnel accused of My Lai massacre (2)/Wikimedia Commons; p. 46 Armed Forces Full Honor Wreath-laying Ceremony in honor of the 50th anniversary of the end of the Vietnam War at the Vietnam Veteran's Memorial in Washington on April 25, 2025 - 8/Wikimedia Commons; p. 47 zijin/Shutterstock.com; p. 51 Joaquin Ossorio Castillo/Shutterstock.com; p. 52 ItzaVU/Shutterstock.com; p. 53 Ceremony honoring Vietnam War veterans at the Vietnam Veterans Memorial in Washington, March 29, 2025 - 3/Wikimedia Commons; p. 54 Anton_Ivanov/Shutterstock.com.

ABOUT THE AUTHOR

NICOLE HORNING is a published author of several nonfiction books for children and teens. She has her bachelor's degree in English and a master's degree in education. She doesn't just write for a living; she also enjoys it as a hobby. Nicole loves to collect books and read anything that sounds interesting to her. She also loves learning new things, especially historical topics. She does her best work while listening to Taylor Swift and having one of her two cats in her lap—both things happen a lot.